*The*

# WELL-SET TABLE

# THE WELL-SET

# T·A·B·L·E

## Ryan Gainey

*Written with Frances Schultz*

*Photography by David Schilling*

TAYLOR PUBLISHING COMPANY

DALLAS, TEXAS

ALSO BY RYAN GAINEY

*The Well-Placed Weed*

Published by Taylor Publishing Company
1550 West Mockingbird Lane
Dallas, Texas 75235

Sunflower painting, p. v, by Jenny Fitch.

Designed by David Timmons

**Library of Congress Cataloging-in-Publication Data**
Gainey, Ryan.
    The well-set table / Ryan Gainey, written with Frances Schultz :
photography by David Schilling.
        p.        cm.
    ISBN 0-87833-945-0
    I. Table setting and decoration.  I. Schultz, Frances, 1957–
II. Title.
TX897.G35  1996
642'.8—DC20                                              96–31768
                                                            CIP

Printed in the United States of America

10      9      8      7      6      5      4      3      2      1

*To my dear friend Jenny Fitch.*

A great gardener, a great cook, and an extraordinary woman
whose life made us smile.

# ᔧ The Subjects ᔧ

Prologue                                                          1

Artichokes and Pomegranates                                      3

Olives                                                           21

Turnips, Sweet Potatoes, and Chinaberries                       33

Lemon Thyme and Lemon Balm                                      49

Queen Anne's Lace and Wild Blackberries                         65

Sunflowers and Tomatoes                                         77

Corn                                                            93

Palms                                                          113

Grapes                                                         125

Bulbs and Pines                                                135

Acknowledgments                                                158

# ✙ PROLOGUE ✙

*B*efore all else temporal, I love the earth. It has given me not only
life, but my life's work—and my bliss. That is what my first book,
*The Well-Placed Weed*, was about. I find it deeply gratifying now that
gardening has taken hold in our lives with such fervor. I think we
are literally pushing our souls out of the ground, and I rejoice to hear people
talking about the land again, in many contexts. ✿ The earth, and her seasons,
are constantly supplying us with a source of food. Man, in domesticating these
sources, has taken nature and turned it into art. Not only the food we eat and
dishes we prepare, but every single thing that we call art has come out of the
earth—whether a painting, or a mosaic, or a beautiful bowl, or a piece of
jewelry or flatware. Every pigment, every piece of wood, every bit of clay,
stone, and metal—all are of the earth. Even the stories we tell—man's earliest
myths and memories—are inevitably entwined with nature because so was man
himself, at least until he learned to separate from it so effectively. Each of us
needs to unveil our memory, pull the books off the shelf and reunite our souls
with the myths that are essential to the reality of planting our dreams. ✿
*The Well-Set Table* is not a departure but an extension of what the earth and her
resources offer us. I hope that in creating beauty we also create awareness. I
hope these pages will affirm for you that a well-set table and a meal brought to
it, be they simple or grand, are stories in the telling—the culmination of an
entire process of history, of horticulture, of gastronomy. The table is not just
about the food we share but about that which we share spiritually—the bread
of life. And in so doing, we experience, at its simplest and most profound, the
continuity of growth and the joy of life, in this great garden we call humanity.

# ARTICHOKES ❧ AND ❧ POMEGRANATES

Table settings that take their cues from themes and seasonal occasions are well and good, but they do risk running into clichés. Sometimes a table setting is a process—a creative synthesis of all sorts of events and influences—some deliberate and contrived, some serendipitous. Being open to them encourages not only inspiration but originality. ❋ A fundraising ball I designed for the Atlanta Botanical Garden had a Scottish theme. Research on Scottish history and Celtic lore led me to the thistle, for which I've had a longstanding love, and it was as if the plant's beautiful and delicate spines pointed to one idea after another. The ball was a wonderful memory, and I wanted to create a dinner with all I learned from it. ❋ From the thistle and its close kin the artichoke, we had plates, glasses and napery designed, handpainted, etched, and even beaded. Then we added the ruby-seeded pomegranate and the season's last, still-green tomatoes, including the exalted with the lowly and allowing all to contribute. It made for a rich harmony of autumn jewel-toned colors. ❋ All of these things constantly come to me, not necessarily by choice but by looking, listening, reading, and being aware—and all are brought to fruition simply by having good food.

A garland festooning the mirror is made from dried artichokes, pomegranates, pine cones, oak, and lemon leaves. The handpainted tablecloth and napkins carry the theme further. Muslin draping the walls gives the room softness and warmth.

La Artichoke
Napkin
Folding Instructions
(optional of course)

...ding front side.

...sewing

$\mathcal{I}$ nspired by the dinner's theme, Julia Junkin designed, sewed, and painted artichoke napkins (and provided instructions for folding them). She created the tablecloth as well.

This thistle sketch inspired accompanying plates and napkins—all in collaboration with Keith Summerour. These exquisitely beaded thistle-motif napkins are the work of Dawn Hutchins Hartman.

The thistle appears
again in etched
glassware made in Mexico.

*A*rtichoke plates
imported from Italy.

The pomegranate reveals its ruby-jeweled inner-structure, a sculpture of nature. The tray is a Guatemalan corn husk tray.

Cordials await filling with grenadine, a digestive divined from the pomegranate.

An antique urn is arranged with artichokes, winter lettuces, and harlequin glory bower.

$\mathcal{A}$ menu inspired by the season and the table setting includes this artichoke and green tomato flan served in a Spanish burlap basket.

$\mathcal{W}$inter lettuces and
endive stuffed with
herbed goat cheese are sprinkled
with a pomegranate vinaigrette.

An Italian glazed terra cotta platter makes a handsome serving piece for the duck comfit and white bean dishes, with green tomatoes as garnish.

*T*he Italian ceramic acorn finial echoes the ochre in the plates and the oak in the garland. A French grape-rinsing basket spills over with green tomatoes and into a Mediterranean dough-rising bowl. The homemade honeysuckle wine is by Brooks Garcia.

Winter lettuces and endive
stuffed with goat cheese

Duck confit with white beans

Artichoke and green tomatoe flan

Pomegranate sorbet

# ❧ OLIVES ❧

In the presentation of food, the sense of smell is as important as the sense of taste, and the scent of an olive grove is the closest thing I know to heaven. In mythology, it was the goddess Athena who gave the olive to man. Man's earliest relationship with nature was based on foraging—fruit, nuts, berries, roots—whatever he could find. What we eat today cannot even be compared to those ancient plants in their wild, original form. What we have today has been domesticated, hybridized, improved. I wonder sometimes if we haven't lost the ability to taste or to appreciate something wild, like the first Europeans in South America must have done, for example. So it is ironic, and somehow pleasing, that the olive—hardly palatable in its natural state—is not likely much different from that which Athena first brought. But to be eaten and enjoyed, it must be cured and preserved, or its oil must be extracted to cook with and use for other things. ❧ Grown in Europe and California, olives share a family of plants whose roots reach to the American South. The rampant, silver-dust-leaved *Elaeagnus angustifolia* has sweetly fragrant blossoms that endear it to the autumn garden. In fact, fall blooming is a wonderful characteristic of this

Robert Mooney made this chandelier of pecan branches intertwined with olive boughs from California. Silver from Beverly Bremer includes poppy salt and pepper shakers, fitting since poppies and olives both grow in Mediterranean climes. Even the tablecloth, actually an old embroidered bedspread, has an olive motif, as do the napkins. The folding screen's panels are of chicken wire stuffed with magnolia and maple leaves by Scott Pluckhahn.

plant family, another familiar Southern member of which is the osmanthus, or tea olive. It, too, is fragrant, though it doesn't produce anything we eat, technically—the Japanese drop the blossoms in their tea so they may take in the fragrance while taking their tea. ❦ Homage to the olive is a way of recognizing our link to other lands and other cultures, and also of honoring its symbol. Athena, its mythological giver, was also the goddess of wisdom, and the olive became the sacred tree of Athens and protector of the warriors. In Biblical times, when Noah's ordeal was nigh ending, he saw a white dove with an olive branch, meaning that somewhere in the world there was something growing, and the earth was saved.

The menu included olives and olive bread, artichokes filled
with olive tapenade and a pâté surrounded with mushrooms
and served in a simple, earthy container made from twigs and bark.
Much of this setting is about food from foraging—things that grow at
the roots of trees, or on them, found in the woods.

$\mathcal{A}$ separate, smaller room was transformed with burlap stapled ceiling-to-wall and the judicious strewing of branches and leaves. The feeling of sanctuary is heightened by the cross sculpture, a rare, nineteenth-century Eastern European work of tramp art made from old cigar boxes. The beautiful olive cake is by Angie Mosier.

The money plant branches shining in the foreground can be grown in any garden. Its botanical name, *Lunaria annua,* alludes to its little moon seed pods, but its other common name, "poor man's money," brings a charming message: if you have nothing else to give, give from the garden. This is a philosophy to keep.

The honour of your presence is requested at the marriage of Andrew Peter and Thomas Chapman... May 26 Roseheam

menu

olives
from la regalido,
provence

olive bread

artichokes
with olive tapenade

red snapper
with tomato salsa

champagne sorbet

# TURNIPS, SWEET POTATOES,
## ❧ AND ❧
## CHINABERRIES

This is all about roots, and I mean both the kind you come from and the kind that you eat. For me—growing up in South Carolina—that means living with the seasons and living off the land. The vegetables we grew to harvest in the fall were root vegetables, including turnips and sweet potatoes, which could be stored for the winter. I remember going out to the field with my Aunt Marie and the mule, and we children would pull the sweet potato vines out of the way of the plow. Then we'd save a sweet potato to root in a glass with water, and the vine—which is in the morning glory family—would grow all the way around the kitchen window. ❧ Unlike the sweet potato, the turnip is an Old World plant. It has the added benefit of producing edible greens, the quality and intensity of which are at their best when they've had just a touch of frost. We'd cook the greens and put the turnips aside to store. In my house, it was my father who reserved the right to cook the greens, and he did them the old-fashioned way with a little fat back or streak o' lean. And my mother would make cornbread for sopping in the pot liquor, which was the liquid left in the pot after cooking the greens. My father worked the second

I've loved marbles ever since I was a child, and we played them constantly in our yard, which was mostly dirt. This quirky chandelier is made from marbles by Jeff Almeida, as were the napkin rings.

shift at the mill, and when he came home he would have cornbread and pot liquor before going to bed. That was his late-night snack. So I decided to have a party honoring my father and what became a little ritual in our family. ❧ It was autumn then, with school in session and Christmas coming. Aside from turnips and sweet potatoes, we had chinaberries, which would drop their fruit at this same time of year. A tree grew in our dirt yard, and we made our sling shots and other toys from it, and it gave us a wonderful fragrance when it bloomed in the spring. We also made necklaces from the berries themselves, by boiling them to remove the fruit, stringing them together, and dyeing them. And these were our mothers' Christmas presents. ❧ As the idea for this gathering developed, one memory seemed to feed into another, until it became almost a re-creation of a time long past. The difference of course is that we are very much in the present, and this was an evening to reminisce, to recall family heritage, to seek a happy memory, and to celebrate.

$\mathscr{A}$ letter from my mother to my father
during World War II, when he was
serving in the Philippines. Memories aren't meant
to be tucked away.

Amid old family photos is a picture of my grandmother in this frame made by Huckleberry Starnes to look like a screen door. Screen doors, and Grandmama Gainey looking through them to keep an eye on us grandchildren, hold a special meaning for me. I don't think I'd live in a house without one.

The meal: turnip greens and pot liquor, poached quail eggs, cornbread, sweet potatoes, and goat cheese encrusted with crushed pecans. Huckleberry also made a table and chairs from bead board and tin, because I grew up pumping water and washing clothes on a scrub board.

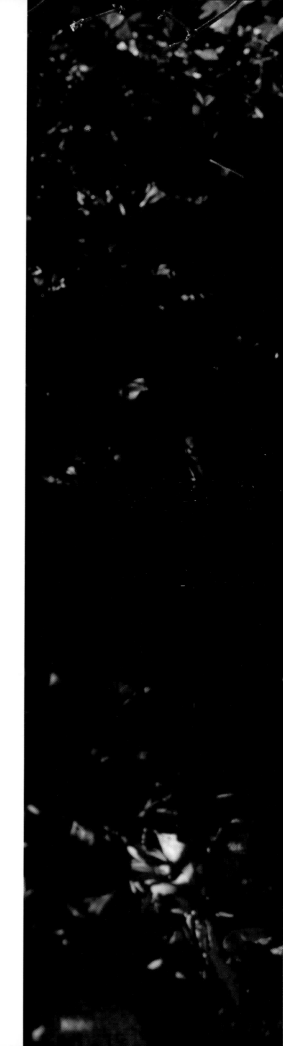

*A* bowl of fruit includes the bumpy but beautifully colored Osage orange, named for the Osage Indians who grew them in the Midwest.

*I*n keeping with American traditions and native American plants, Angie Mosier prepared this cake to look like the stump of a pecan tree.

*C*hinaberry
jewelry
and baubles in
the making laid out
on a Seminole rick-
rack pattern fabric.

*T*he kitchen
pantry, hung
inside with burlap
Christmas stockings
embroidered with
chinaberries.

*A*n old botanical print of an old
Southern botanical icon—the
chinaberry tree. This is a tree I grew up
with, but it also fits into a gentle web of
connections in my life. When I later knew
and pronounced the tree's botanical name,
*Melia azedarach,* it recalled my childhood
fascination with the sound-alike Old
Testament trio Meshach, Shadrach, and
Abednego. Unite with these names the
"rick-rack" of the Seminole fabric—I have
an affinity for their work—and you have
a merry group of rhymes. These are the
kinds of connections—sound, visual,
all the senses—that life offers us if
we look.

$\mathcal{P}$urists will tell you an iron skillet is
the only thing to cook cornbread in.

# LEMON THYME
## ✣ AND ✣
# LEMON BALM

The true meaning of "Epicurean" derives from the idea of enjoying everything you eat—and that doesn't always mean vast amounts of food. Sometimes it can be very little, consumed not for the sake of consumption, but for the sake of the essence of life. That essence, or some aspect of it, can be of your choosing. It may be based on the time of day, or the time of year, or even some fanciful allegory or myth—or a bit of all of those. But you don't have to have everything at once. The idea, such as this setting I created for the Southeastern Flower Show, may be just to have tea and cake. ✣ I love pretty cakes—that's why the artistry of Angie Mosier is so prominent in this book—and it is part of why I'm enthralled with patterns and pattern-making. My mother used to bake cakes for every occasion, and we children loved to help decorate them. We'd mix the butter with the sugar and food coloring, and then we'd have to practice on wax paper before venturing on to the cake itself. For me, those were the beginnings of watching somebody create something beautiful and learning to do it myself. ✣ Tea and cake parties—à la *Alice in Wonderland*—lend themselves to a touch of whimsy, to going beyond the conventional limits of creativity and entering the world of imagination where

Friends and fellow creative spirits Count Beauregard DuBois and Brian Carter came to the end of the rainbow to help build and paint the pop-up garden and house for the Southeastern Flower Show.

everything is possible. This led to our creating a "pop-up" garden, incorporating that which is imaginary and that which is real—and reflecting a lot of ideas about my own house and garden. Pop-up cards were always a source of fascination for me, like the putting together of wonderful pictures and pieces of puzzles—again, my appreciation for patterns and the stories they tell. ॐ Once upon a time, there was a woman who lived in a house at the end of a rainbow. The Rainbow Man came one day to visit and brought her the colors of the rainbow, which came up the next spring in her garden. There were cutouts in fanciful shapes, topiaries, sunflowers, and black-eyed Susans, and little creatures to play among them. There was tea, of course, and lemonade, and tea cake made from lemon thyme and lemon balm—and living happily ever after.

$\mathcal{W}$ hen the Rainbow Man came to call, he brought the colors of the rainbow. The colors came up in the garden, in fanciful cut-outs and flowers, and little creatures came out to play.

An antique wire table was shielded from the sun by a parasol in the shape of a sunflower, made by Jeroy Hannah. A circular form filled with oasis and loosely "planted" with tulips could be illuminated at night by votives in and around the arrangement.

This whimsical and exuberant bird-feeder was painted by the Count.

The cake of lemon thyme and lemon balm was placed on an old glass stand embellished with tiny bouquets of lantana blossoms and lemon balm, a kind of mint. Plates were garnished with baskets fashioned from cut-out lemons, which could be filled with lemon sorbet or some other confection. *Miel de Provence*, honey of Provence, was for sweetening the tea and lemonade.

$\mathcal{A}$ny garden needs the excitement and playfulness of
a dog or two. In the pop-up garden, these wildly
colored carved dogs represent the real thing. They came from
Guatemala.

*P*eeking through the foliage are cats, angels, dogs— representing the naive, whimsical reflections of the heart.

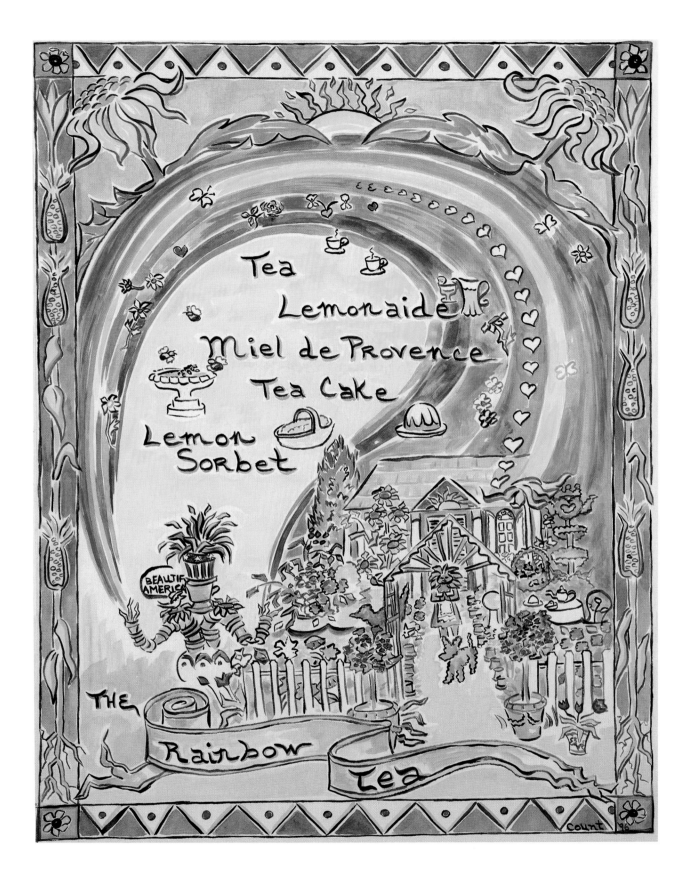

# QUEEN ANNE'S LACE
# ❧ AND ❧
# WILD BLACKBERRIES

*I*f the Queen Anne's lace is in bloom, then you know the wild blackberries are ripe. Have an impromptu celebration, with flower and fruit as the occasion. Queen Anne's lace blooms in early summer, and in the South it seems to be everywhere—in the countryside, along highways, across fallow fields. It would be wonderful just to go out in the middle of it and have a tea party, but that's not very realistic, even for somebody like me. So why not gather a bunch from some field, and cut huge branches of blackberries—which are probably growing rampant somewhere nearby—and bring them home? ❊ We set the table right in the middle of my garden and created a giant parasol to shade it. The true success of arranging flowers is to do them the way they grow. That's why it is so easy to make an umbrella out of Queen Anne's lace, and to entwine the berries—which are really vines—up the shaft. Indeed, the tiny white florets are called *umbels*, whose spoke-like construction resembles that of an umbrella. Most likely the word comes from the Italian *ombrella*, diminutive of *ombra*, from the Latin *umbra*, meaning shadow or shade. ❊ As is often the case, and as I am fond of pointing out in any decoration or design I'm involved with, a pattern from nature may beautifully become a motif for man.

*A* moss-filled basket atop a slender tree trunk anchors the "spokes" of our Queen Anne's lace umbrella in my garden in Decatur, just outside Atlanta. ❊ After tea, a battered blue rocker invites you to while away the afternoon hours in the lengthening shade.

The berries bring things blue, for serving and eating, and "lace" decorates the table in powdered sugar sifted through doilies. The lacy tabletop echoes the pattern of the flower. Blackberry pie and lemonade complete a fine summer's welcome.

*F*resh, wild berries inspire a host of confections— fresh blackberry pie and a cake with blackberry filling created by Angie Bennett Mosier.

*T*he sweet tartness of homemade lemonade is the perfect partner to blackberry pie, and its yellow complements the purply black of the berries and the blue of the tablecloth. A favorite, buggish brooch adds a whimsical touch.

$\mathcal{A}$ ngie's perfect, latticed
pastry makes miniature
frames for berries and leaves.

$\mathcal{A}$ hand-blown, blue glass bowl filled
with water, blossoms and lemon serves
as a community fingerbowl and pretty refreshment
for delicious, sweet stickyness.

*E*ach component of a table setting is like
a note in a symphony. The table setting
is a composition, a work of art.

$\mathcal{I}$ just happened to have these
reticulated plates that resemble
the structure of Queen Anne's lace—it's like
looking up into an open umbrella.

# SUNFLOWERS
❧ A N D ❧
## TOMATOES

Flowers and fruits of the garden, and man's relationship to them, are part of our mythology and therefore shape our culture and our lives. The Native American story of the sunflower—akin to the Biblical version of the Flood—is one with which I identify on several levels. It speaks to me through my Cherokee heritage and through the simple joy of the flower itself. ❀ There was a time when the Great Creator became angry with the people because they were not taking care of the earth, so he sent a flood. Mother Sun, in fear and frustration, beseeched the creator to cease, that she might get on with her work of warming and drying the earth. A tiny and not significant star called Bright Star loved Mother Sun dearly and wanted to help, but Mother Sun told her there was nothing she could do. Bright Star in turn pleaded with Great Creator, who was so moved by the little star's devotion that he turned her into a seed and planted her. The rains stopped, and the seed grew and flowered in the shape of the sun. And the flower loved Mother Sun so much that

What man has extracted from nature in order to beautify the world in which he lives is phenomenal—a beautiful plate to eat from, a glass to drink with, and a table to set them on. It's really just a matter of deciding to do it—to beautify your own life that way.

it followed her throughout the day and bowed its head in sadness at night. In the early morning, as the last of her dewy tears dry, she lifts her head to greet another day. The Indians found a use for every part of the sunflower, and I have adopted it as the symbol of my business and incorporated it into our logo. ❋ The sunflower can be cultivated in its purest and most basic form—one of those flowers that falls into the old-timey category called "cut and come again"—like zinnias and cosmos—and like tomatoes. The more you pick, the more they produce, until the season wanes and you let the plants mature and save the seed. ❋ Tomatoes and sunflowers are one of nature's most vivid color combinations, and, fortuitously, a simultaneous one. When the sunflowers are blooming, tomatoes are ripe for the picking. Interestingly, this bulbous red icon of Italian cuisine did not originate in Europe but in the Americas, and was introduced to the Continent by early explorers. The history of plants is the history of man, and man is always seeking new things to grow and to eat. ❋ A menu full of the flavors of summer is prepared and served with pieces that repeat and echo patterns of the flowers and fruit themselves.

The menu included a molded pesto rice salad encrusted with crushed, roasted sunflower seeds; a goat cheese and tomato flan; fresh butterbeans with steamed okra; a tomato and onion tart; fresh sliced tomatoes, of course; and fresh peas and lettuces from the garden.

The table setting—including
the table itself—harmoniously
continues the patterns of the plants and
flowers themselves. These ceramic plates
were created by Bob Francisco
in an adaptation of our logo. Shatzi
McLean created the mosaic tabletop from
pottery shards inlaid with my plates.

*T*his terra cotta
putto, with his
offering of cherry tomatoes,
seems to approve of the
proceedings.

*A* cool blue is the perfect foil to hot summer reds and yellows. This bench offers homemade goodies—more of summer's bounty.

This is a kind of
"Pomedoro's Box" that,
opened, reveals "apples of love"
(the translation of the Italian
name for tomato) and a small,
prized vessel of Balsamic vinegar.
Bob Francisco painted this handsome wooden box that picks up
the mosaic motif.

This platter of field peas is garnished with basil that's rather special. It's *Basilica rustica*, the common basil of Italy, and I grew it from seed collected there on a trip. A treasure such as this, hand-carried from afar, enhances the table. It's charming to know that the only way to have it is to have been there, seen it, and procured it.

*I*talian peach tea is the perfect, sweet, refreshing counterpoint to our summer feast. It is made with imported tea, dried peach, *limone* (an Italian liqueur), and my own fresh Georgia peaches.

*B*utter-beans, okra, and a perfect, scene-stealing sunflower blossom.

*F*resh sliced tomatoes—could it be summer without them?—create a new kind of blossom, with a seed head at the center.

the menu
pesto rice salad
goat cheese and tomato flan
fresh butter beans with okra
tomato and onion tart
fresh tomatoes with greens
hog apple pie

# ❧ CORN ❧

orn is probably one of the most important culinary elements in the Americas; like the sunflower, it provides a source of food—not only for man but for the animals man needs to plow the fields and work the land. ❧ It is also one of the oldest crops in cultivation and one of the earliest examples of man's ability to make natural selections and hybrids. Farmers of ages past were able to hold the corn in their hands and identify the variations occurring with cross-pollination. Back then corn was bred to be short to keep the wind from blowing it over. The corn plants we're accustomed to in North America are relatively new. They are also taller, owing to milder weather here than in Central and South America. ❧ Short or tall, corn has always been grown in rows, unlike wheat and barley, for example, whose tiny seeds were broadcast by hand. Corn, much larger by comparison, was planted in long furrows that follow the pattern of the plant—uniform rows of glistening white, yellow, or blue kernels. And like other crops of the ancient world, corn and its cultivation were revered, giving rise to worship, song and dance, and hence civilization itself. It also had a lot to do with the artistic expression of the Indians, inspiring them to do beadwork and mosaics resembling the patterns of the

The evening's menu consisted of creamed corn chowder with potatoes and cumin (all native to the Americas), grits cooked in goat cheese and garlic, quail wrapped in country ham with arugula, tomatoes and okra, and cornbread.

plants and kernels. ❧ As the season progresses, the bounty of the garden grows. Midsummer is a busy time for gardeners because not only are we harvesting, we are beginning to store for the winter—canning and freezing what isn't eaten. In antiquity, waste was a punishable crime; in today's world, conservation is noble. ❧ The growing, cooking, canning, creaming and eating of corn still resonates with me from my background in an agrarian family. The process and the ritual surrounding it are as nurturing to the human spirit as the food we eat is to our bodies. ❧ So I wanted to have a party to celebrate the fact that corn was in season. And most Southerners who grew up with it know that the best corn is picked about thirty minutes before dinner and quickly boiled, so as not to lose one grain of its essence!

The table is draped in a handpainted cloth by Julia Junkin, lit by a Moravian star and corn-shaped candles.

This basket is crafted of succulents by Mary Ann Gatlin. The fruit-laden Mexican lanterns were painted by Bob Francisco.

*J*ulia Junkin also created the exquisite napkins to emulate ears of corn, replete with "corn silk" fringe. The blue glasses were a last-minute flea market find. The soup bowls are Provençal, and the chargers and inner bowls are by Westmore Pottery in North Carolina.

*B*ob Francisco painted the extraordinary mosaics on a series of plates, and I collaborated with Rugs by Robinson on the needlepointed sunflower design of the carpet shown here in the background.

*O*ld World and New World unite
botanically here, with the grape and
the sunflower combined. These flora twine
around Dionysus, that Old World god.

For this occasion, we made a shrine to Native Americans. The Nez Percé tribe in particular was admired for its corn husk handiwork, which can be seen at the back of this cabinet—an early twentieth-century piece from Ohio that sports an unusual corn motif in its pierced tinwork panels.

Crowning our shrine is an old Mason jar filled with moonshine and peach juice that we picked up at dawn at the Madison County Line.

ornmeal, homemade breads, honey, and other products of the harvest await on a rustic pantry table.

$\mathcal{T}$he cornbread was baked in special decorative molds—nineteenth-century ironstone molds—then served as dessert with cream and molasses.

An antique beaded Paiute gathering bag is from my collection of Native American artifacts.

# PALMS

All of us arise—emotionally and creatively—from whence we came. Though most of us nowadays don't live in the same place where we grew up, we still have memories of our first homes and where our first meals were. I've lived in Georgia for twenty years, but I am a native South Carolinian, and I am always glad when my work takes me back there—which it has many times. Recently I was asked to create a party for the patrons of Brookgreen Gardens, on the coast near Litchfield, South Carolina. One of my first garden experiences as a child was on a field trip to those gardens—and I really have no memory of it except that I went. It was so big and I was so small…But I came to appreciate Brookgreen tremendously. For this very special party, I wanted to bring everything that was part of the garden into one fold. ❧ Developed in the 1930s by railroad heir Archer Huntington and his wife, Brookgreen is laid out in the classical manner with a series of garden "rooms," the overall pattern of which suggests the shape of a butterfly. The house, inspired by the architecture of the Spanish Mediterranean, is named *Atalaya*, which is Spanish for "watch tower." The feeling is of a place that

Recognizing the home state of Brookgreen Gardens, the table decorations took cues from the South Carolina state flag. For tablecloths and napkins, Julia Junkin handpainted palmetto palms and crescent moons against blue sky and sandy beach. Tropical flora were integrated with Spanish moss and branches of oak, pine, and dogwood to create informal centerpieces appropriate to the coastal setting.

has belonged there for centuries. All plant material is native, and the mile-long allée of palm trees that once led to the house is in the process of being restored. ✌ It was the graceful and statuesque palmetto—the South Carolina state tree—that held such appeal. The state flag depicts a palmetto, silhouetted by the light of a crescent moon, on a midnight blue ground, and we incorporated these symbols—and other South Carolina motifs—into the theme of the evening. Tablecloths were handpainted with palmettos, moons, dunes, and the ocean. The plates were yellow as a summer sun, decorated with sea shells and starfish. Glassware was clear ocean blue. Napkins were inscribed with lines from Shelley's poem "The Cloud," an amusement for guests to assemble the phrases' sequence and a nod to the poetry-inscribed plaques and rocks one finds placed along Brookgreen's sandy paths and walkways. ✌ The menu, too, was of the South Carolina coast—shrimp, catfish, quail, and salt-cured ham, garnished with coneflower seed heads and the vivid orange fruit from the palms. ✌ Dessert was served in the courtyard, where tables were adorned with dogwood branches, pine boughs, and palm fronds. This again emphasized the idea of the gardens and their native flora, so we decorated the cakes as well in oak, dogwood, pine, and palmetto designs. It was twilight by then, and the courtyard was illuminated by hundreds of twinkling votives. As the guests strolled in, a perfect crescent moon rose in the sky to welcome them.

*I am the daughter of Earth and Water,*
*And the nursling of the Sky;*
*I pass through the pores of the ocean and shores;*
*I change, but I cannot die.*

From "The Cloud"

The plates, created by
Liz Quackenbush, were
bright as the summer
sun. Glassware was
washed in the
colors of
the sea.

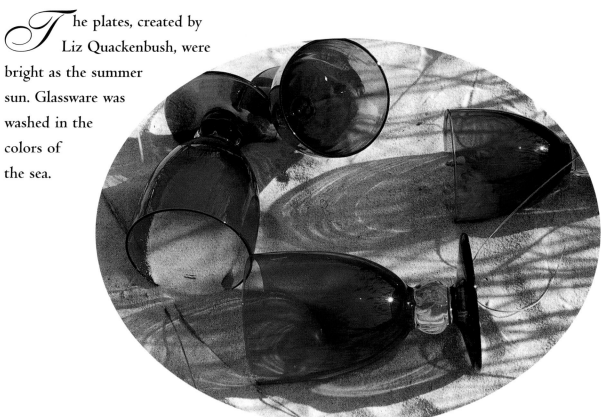

*T*he courtyard at *Atalaya*.

*A*talaya, the house built by Archer Huntington and his wife in 1932, as seen through the dunes, from the ocean.

*A* Low Country
shrimp boil is
garnished with coneflower
seed heads.

*F* ried tomatoes and catfish.

$\mathcal{Q}$uail wrapped in salt-
cured ham and grits
cakes with goat cheese and
garlic were a Southern and
satisfying main course.

# ❧ GRAPES ❧

As a horticulturist, my life's work is of the earth—the process by which living things grow and the seasons by which growing things live. It is also the source of my creativity, rooted in contemplation of man's relationship with nature. Since the dawn of time that relationship has been expressed in myths, fables, even religious ceremonies, that revolve around the seasons and the cultivation of plants for food. 🍇 In Egyptian mythology there is the Green Man, the archetype of man as caretaker of the earth and cultivator of life. The Romans had Bacchus, and the Greeks had Dionysus, who taught man to grow the grape and to distill its spirits. Their stories are all connected, as all share ideas and principles constituting universal truths, and they have relevance to our lives today. Finally, we've become aware of the need to preserve and conserve just as we're on the verge of destroying the very things—the forest, the ocean, the atmosphere— we've been given to take care of, and to take care of us. It's as if the Green Man has appeared again to remind us that civilization must not remove itself too far from the land. 🍇 A form of the Green Man, I believe, is Dionysus, and I've chosen Dionysus to celebrate with this dinner. Because while he, like the Green Man, is about cultivation and preservation, he is also about revelry and wine—

On a circular table in the visitor's garden, Andrew Crawford hand-wrought this iron canopy draped with inexpensive bleached muslin and voile and trimmed in cotton fringe and grapevines—scuppernongs from my garden. Autumn-blooming white hydrangeas crown the canopy's swags. Limiting the colors to white and green cools off the heat of Indian summer.

and this, after all, is a party. 🍇 The time of year is the autumnal equinox, sig-
nifying the end of one season and the beginning of another. In antiquity, it
was also the time of the Dionysan festival, a celebration of harvest and bounty
and of grapes and wine. The legendary festival included a ceremonial dance,
performed in the round amid a circle of grapevines. The circle, with no beginning and no end, bespoke the continuous cycles of the harvest and of life. 🍇
As a symbol, the circle is as appropriate for an ancient ceremony as for its
modern-day derivation, like the one we've prepared here. In my "visitor's garden," which is in a circle, we have a circular table, dressed in a canopy of white
and vines, with the centerpiece an abundance of grapes. Of course this might
be used for any occasion—an engagement or wedding, for example, whereby
man and woman come together to bring forth their own fruit, to produce yet
another generation of caretakers for the earth. 🍇 We have so much to pull
from in our own culture. While we create beauty, we may also create awareness.
And in so doing, we experience, at its simplest and most profound, the continuity of growth and the joy of life.

$\mathcal{A}$lisa Barry of Bella
Cucina prepared a
menu of salmon with a basil pesto
sauce, preceded by a pasta course
and followed by a salad of beets
with fresh herbs and greens.
Dessert was lemon sorbet with
biscotti and an Angie Mosier cake.

*A*ngie Mosier created a magnificent cake draped with bunches of grapes.

The dinner plates were made by a potter in North Carolina—to have something from the earth, from somewhere around us. We also used French pottery with a grape design. If you have your grandmother's silver or china, use it. Don't put it away in a cabinet—that's not the point of having it. This beautiful flatware with the grape motif was loaned by Beverly Bremer.

*A* golden Bacchus upholds the goblets to be filled with his sacred libation.

*Fauns with youthful Bacchus follow;*
*Ivy crowns that brow supernal*
*As the forehead of Apollo,*
*And possessing youth eternal.*

*Round about him, fair Bacchantes,*
*Bearing cumbals, flutes, and thyrses,*
*Wild from Naxian groves, or Zante's*
*Vineyards, sing delirious verses.*

Henry Wadsworth Longfellow,
from "Drinking Song"

*G*lass-beaded grapes form delicate clusters encircling the napkins.

# BULBS
### ❧ AND ❧
# PINES

*E*dible bulbs are the final dip into the storage bin, the end of one season and the clearing for another. Most of us think of bulbs as flowers—daffodils, tulips, hyacinths—for decorative purposes. Rarely do we think of those we eat. But onions are bulbs—chives, scallions, leeks, Vidalias. And so are the many kinds of garlic, including what we call "old society garlic," which grows wild here in the South, and whose tiny purple and white flowers are edible, as are the wild green onions that peskily volunteer in our lawns. These are not flashy or fancy foods, but our appreciation of them has to do with a reverence for simple things. ❀ A bulb, in its simplest and unadorned state, is a vessel for storage. It is a perfectly sculpted series of overlapping scales or leaves, which store the food for the plant inside. Each is a little miracle of nature's patterning and wholeness, as we see when we cut an onion in half and see circle within circle within circle. The word "onion," in fact, derives from a Greek word meaning "one-ness." ❀ When the world inside the bulb begins to awaken, the world outside feels the energy of spring. We're on the verge of the vernal equinox, and the greening season is upon us. The potatoes and onions in your pantry may be sprouting.

*P*ine is a part of Southern heritage, here beautifully crafted by Robert Cox in table and chairs of planks salvaged from an old barn. The bowls are pine as well, hand-carved in Mexico. Ornithogalums arranged in clay pots and wrapped with raffia are dramatic, but simple, decoration.

Outdoors, the first buds peek out from tree branches. And in the South, the pines begin to bloom. ❧ So much of the Southern culture and way of life relates to the pine tree. When I was a little boy we used turpentine for everything, from thinning paint to sterilizing our scraped knees (as if they weren't stinging enough). In the spring I used to forage for fresh pine nuts; there's no better taste in the world. And as an element of architecture and design, the pine is pervasive—from the most modest old country houses, like the one I grew up in, to the finely crafted furniture of salvaged heart pine, like the table and chairs we've used in this setting. For this occasion I even carried the pine a step further to incorporate its etymological kin, the pineapple, so-called for its resemblance to the pine cone. As the worldwide symbol of hospitality, the pineapple is welcome in any context of entertaining. ❧ For me, the meaning of this and every table setting is that each has a story and entails the passing on of knowledge—an understanding of what we come from and who we are. The well-set table, ideally, is recognition that the meal brought to it and the company around it are the culmination of an entire process, historically, horticulturally, and gastronomically. It is the final and gratifying stage not just about the food we share but about that which we share spiritually—the bread of life. We store it in our bodies, and in our souls, and we must always put something aside for the year to come—and for the next generations.

*I*n the centerpiece, "bulbs" growing in a Moroccan brazier were filled with sautéed pearl onions and golden raisins. Flanking the centerpiece, shallots and pearl onions stuck with toothpicks ring the bases of ornithogalum stems in hand-made terra cotta English bulb pots.

longside plain glasses of iced tea are exotic, hand-polished gourds, used by South American Indians for drinking *atole*, a nourishing liquid made from finely ground corn. A round of pinenutty bread accompanies a hearty first course of bean and pasta soup.

$\mathcal{A}$lliums, narcissus,
ornithogalums, and
agapanthus—all bulbs—rise from
a circle of moss and laurel leaves.

*O*rnithogalum blossums and a
garlic bulb adorn a dish of garlic flan. Wendy Reinstein prepared this
and more of our feast.

This onion tart finds a lovely home in Bob Francisco's hand-painted sunflower platter.

nions sautéed with fresh herbs.

*J*n a pine needle basket, pearl onions, allium, and sunflower petals top sundried tomatoes and polenta.

*A* collection of baskets and blossoms in the sitting room—and collections of other things all around the house—need not just sit and be dusted. Bring them to the table and use them!

These baskets represent all the different cultures of the American South—new and old—and all feature longneedled pine in their construction. The chain links them together.

*N*ative American baskets and terra
cotta sculpture could be on the
mantle one day and dinner table the next.
This painting by the Count is a whimsical
rendition of the front of my house and
garden in Decatur, near Atlanta.

$\mathcal{S}$alt-cured ham with home-grown Swiss chard and leeks. This enticing dish is presented in a magnificent nineteenth-century Turkish serving piece of hand-wrought copper that has been placed in an Afghan basket. The basket's cover continues the geometric theme of the background fabric.

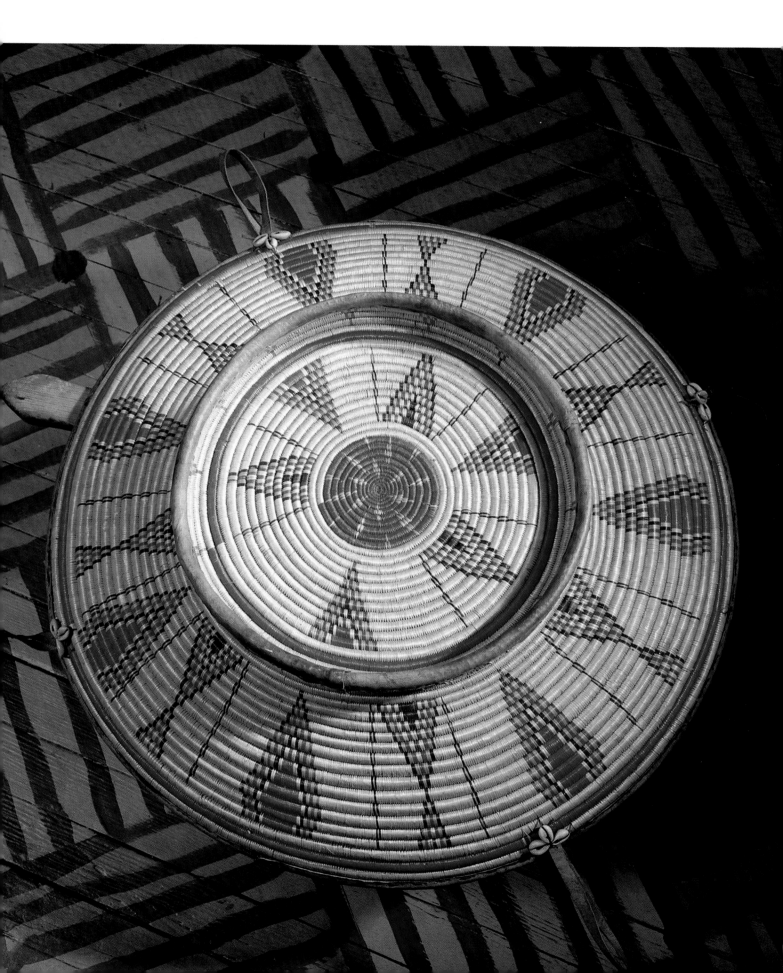

*B*read pudding a-bloom with daffodils and vanilla beans in a laurel wreath. Each daffodil cup is filled with mead, an Old World libation of fermented honey and water.

Menu !!!

Bean and Pasta soup
   w/ Pine nut bread
Garlic flan, onion tart
   & polenta
Salt cured ham w/
   Swiss chard
Bread pudding

SUMMEROUR  5·6·96

*W*e originally set the table outside and decked the arbor with boughs of laurel. Swags of garlic, onions, and corn completed the setting—but spring showers that day drowned it out.

*A* "washing-up"
basin was set
outside for guests.

# Acknowledgments

To give proper credit to all those who helped make this book would be a tough task, since the number is endless. But I do want to thank everyone who has touched my life with teaching, understanding, and most importantly sharing the essential elements of living.

Still, it is Mother Nature who has been my greatest inspiration. Like any great teacher, she taught me the beauty of simplicity. Some of the table settings in this book may seem to challenge the notion of simplicity, but I could not leave out the infinite details so important to making a good setting. I must also thank my garden, which provided the venue for so many of the settings in this book and which continuously nourishes my soul.

The collaborative spirit of artisans and craftsmen is integrated throughout this book, and I would like to thank them collectively, along with all of my staff, my co-writer Frances Schultz, my photographer David Schilling, and my editor Holly McGuire. Only with their help could the well-set tables of my imagination be offered to you in the form of this book.

I would like to thank the chefs Kristen Berney, Alisa Berry, Gary Coley, Vagn Nielsen, Wendy Reinstein, and Marie Addison Lee for the hog-apples; Sara Holcombe Rainey and Hazel Holcombe Johnson for the hog-apple treats; David Dempsey for the lard biscuits; Irene Brown for the moonshine; Rick Berry and Marc Richardson for the frying pan and pot liquor; James M. Moye for the freshest cornmeal on the market; and the gardens of Arvel and Louise Dempsey and Frances and Winslow Howard for their favorite homegrown Rutgers tomatoes. Bob Francisco loaned numerous accessories to the table settings—some of which I keep hoping he won't retrieve! Mary Lou Castle created the exquisite chinaberry jewelry. Angie Tyner surrendered treasures from her travels. Ray Belcher enhanced my Indian basket collection for a few moments, then insisted that I couldn't live without them (an old trick of his). Brian Carter offered sound advice, and on more than one occasion helped me vary the scenes in my house, awakening its ability to change.

Tablecloths are not essential for a plain wooden table or a patch of grass, but they are inviting accessories on which I seem to thrive. What is a tablecloth other than a covering to add ambiance to the theme or motif of a moment? Rugs, shawls, quilts, linens, sacks, cottons, hand-stitched precious heirlooms—the sources are endless. As endless as my luck and gratitude for finding Julia Junkin of Seattle, Washington, whom I have never met, but who created, after countless phone conversations and faxes, so many of the gorgeous hand-painted tablecloths and napkins featured in this book.

Rosemary Steifel captured the creative process through her delicate brush portraits of the table settings. Throughout the making of this book, this good friend shared with me memories of wonderful family food. She decided to turn the collection of her watercolors into a limited edition, which are available through the Ryan Gainey Collection. The collection also includes the della Robbia-inspired wreaths of Native American fruits, vegetables, and other plants, which will be hand-carved in Italy.

For most of us, no meal is complete without good bread and good desserts, and Angie Mosier lovingly prepared the baked delights that accompany the settings in this book. For every subject that was brought to fruition, she was a part of the process—not only of baking and making, but of sharing ideas. She was with me at most of the photography sessions and added her own sense of style to the settings. Her smile and enduring charm made all the work seem more pleasant. She is collaborating with me even now, as we produce an edible dessert parterre for the International Olympic Committee opening party for the 1996 Olympic Games held in Atlanta.

Menu cards are the tangible memories of good meals and well-set tables—lingering awhile to be part of a scrapbook of good times. Scott Pluckhahn, Bob Thomas, Bob Francisco, Rosemary Steifel, The Count, and Keith Summerour prepared the billets du fêtes and collaborated with me on the final, essential details.

The making of this book has been one of the most fulfilling ventures in my work thus far. Its storytelling, its myths, the meaning of words, the capturing of light (be it from candle or sun), the reading of texts, the poem that may be read, or the prayer that is uttered are all a part of the soul that has nurtured my table.

As I labored with ideas and subjects, one person shared with me the vision that I had in creating these table settings—in a manner that only one kindred spirit can share with another. Bob Francisco painted urns, plates, and boxes; cooked; lent; and gave with joy the friendship that good food is all about. I gave him the subject, he turned it into art. His unique style made me continue to create more settings just so I could see his accompanying work. He designed place settings using oak and acorn, grape and vine, pine and cone, and artichoke as motifs, all of which are dear to my heart. His mosaic sunflower and corn plates are treasures to me.

For the opening of the Rings Exhibit to be held during the Olympiad in Atlanta, he is now painting a scene on a folding screen depicting the homage we all must give to life. The main body of the screen depicts a temple at its apex and olive groves and vineyards as part of the landscape, and the panels accompanying this scene depict topiaried peach trees laden with fruit. Here Bob is able to capture that which we all must acknowledge and celebrate: the bounty of the earth. Like the sun that brings forth this bounty has Bob been steadfast with me. I thank him for his friendship, for it is true friendship that we share at our table.